BOLD KIDS

Grand Canyon For Kids

CHILDREN'S BOOKS ON THE USA

No part of this book may be reproduced or used in any way or form or by any means whether electronic or mechanical, this means that you cannot record or photocopy any material ideas or tips that are provided in this book.
Copyright 2022

All images in this book have been reproduced with the knowledge and prior consent of the artists concerned, and no responsibility is accepted by producer, publisher, or printer for any infringement of copyright or otherwise, arising from the contents of this publication.

There are many interesting facts about the Grand Canyon for kids. This magnificent place is the largest canyon in the world, and is much larger than the State of Rhode Island. The most popular attraction in the Grand Canyon is the skywalk, which is the tallest man-made structure in the world.

The Grand Canyon was created by the Colorado River, which started at the west end of the canyon about five million years ago and flowed towards the north. When the river slowed, it carved the canyon, and today you can see its deep gorge.

The river was so powerful, it eroded the rock to create this incredible wonder. There are many interesting facts about the Grand Crater for kids to learn.

While most visitors are fascinated by the grand canyon's size, they are often surprised to discover that it is home to human life. The Havasupai Indian Reservation, which contains the Grand Canyon, has only a population of 208 people.

In fact, this is the most remote community in the lower 48 states. Mail is still delivered to this remote area using pack mule, which makes it a prime example of the Great Unconformity.

The rocks that form the Canyon are 2 billion years old. This is the oldest rock in the canyon and is made from limestone and sandstones. It is incredibly diverse in its features, and is home to many species of animals, including dinosaurs.

It has a fascinating history, and is one of the most popular attractions in the United States. There are several interesting facts about the Grand Crater that kids will love to learn.

The Colorado River is a copper-colored canyon. It is the largest of the seven wonders of the world. The Canyon was carved by the Colorado River about 5 million years ago. While the grand Canyon is not as deep as many people believe, the beautiful colors are a major draw.

If you're planning to visit the park, it's a good idea to read up on it. It's also a great way to learn more about the history of the area.

The Canyon is 2 billion years old. The rocks in the Canyon were formed by erosion. The water stopped forming 230 million years ago, and the Colorado River is over 230 million years old.

The area was named the Grand-Canyon in 1891 by John Wesley Powell, a famous navigator on the Colorado River. It was carved from the river and is one of the most popular sites in the US.

The Canyon was named by the Paiute Indian tribe Kaibab. The name relates to the creamy white limestone that forms the canyon's walls. It's more than 230 million years old!

The Colorado River was carved out of the Canyon 5 million years ago. The river started at the west end and deposited the sediments on the west side, leaving a valley with a steep rock face.

The Grand Canyon is a natural wonder. It was carved by the Colorado River millions of years ago. The river is over 6,000 feet deep and is filled with diverse landscapes. In fact, the floor of the Canyon is one of the coldest places in the lower 48 states.

The rocks here are called strata, and are more than 200 million years old. The gorge is the largest in the United States and is considered one of the Seven Wonders of the World.

Ingram Content Group UK Ltd.
Milton Keynes UK
UKHW050818190723
425402UK00007B/30